RESURRECTING THE BUTTERFLY GRAVEYARD

SARAH ELIZABETH BEACH

ISBN 979-8-88616-607-1 (paperback)
ISBN 979-8-88616-608-8 (digital)

Christian Faith Publishing
832 Park Avenue
Meadville, PA 16335
www.christianfaithpublishing.com

Printed in the United States of America

To my kind, compassionate, and very patient mother. For hours and hours, she sits on the phone with me, listening to me talk. She always offers a loving ear and strong encouragement. My mother has a faith in God that is beautiful, intimate, and powerful. She truly fears the Lord, and her life demonstrates it wonderfully. I would not be who I am today if it was not for her constantly fighting for me.

Also, to my sister, my dad, my close friends, and my family. I will forever love each of you and will always appreciate everything you have done for me.

CONTENTS

ACKNOWLEDGMENTS

For those who were with me during one of the worst seasons of my life and never let me walk alone, I can never thank you enough. You were at my side during my battle with anorexia, all my panic attacks, and every helpless moment of pain. You were with me at every step I took growing closer to Jesus and learning to believe my worth. You were there when I finally let the shawl of shame be ripped from my shoulders. I love you so much, and I appreciate everything you do for me.

Thank you to my dad, Richard Beach, for the cover design and artwork. Also, thank you to Kathryn Young for her editorial assistance, writing mentorship, and friendship. You both made the book happen.

PROLOGUE

Everyone has that moment you never forget, a moment where you're the happiest you've ever been. You're living carefree with the people you love, but then something happens, tainting the memory forever. What once brought so much joy and happiness, now is filled with trauma and agony. You look back on it with a half-smile or maybe even a tear because you know things will never be the same again. You remember all the laughter, the conversations, the adventures, and the ones you spent those moments with. You also remember all the tears, the arguments, the fear, and the challenges after. It's dumbfounding how one moment can bring out two very different emotions. What can be beautiful and free at the time now haunts with an abundance of pain and heartache.

Memories like these are what define us. They're building blocks that make us who we are, either good or bad. The people we experience these moments with will forever be etched into our brains and associated with emotions. Is it fair for those people? Honestly, I have no idea. What I do know is that it happens whether we like it or not. There's a tension that is paralyzing when not only remembering the good times but also accepting things will never be the same because of pain and tragedy.

Sometimes it's not even the particular event we hold on to, but it's the smaller moments leading up to it and the aftermath that follows. The story of the Butterfly Graveyard used to be my favorite memory, but now it serves as a metaphor for me. There can be a sense of freedom and peace in something as horrifying as a graveyard. In life, there are good and bad, but they aren't always segregated. Sometimes they're one and the same. Butterflies live a life like this. They must endure the life of a caterpillar, subjected to the prison of a cocoon before they can freely flap their wings. But even after meta-morphosis, they still die. Life happens, and they're gone. What then? This is the story of resurrecting the Butterfly Graveyard.

Chapter 1

A Wounded Butterfly Falling to the Cold, Hard Ground

MY WORDS

My words encompass all my thoughts.
My words convey every single one of my feelings.
My words show where I am in my journey.
My words tell my whole story.

My words reflect my joy and my anxiety.
My words cut my own throat and stab my own back.
My words reveal my redemption and my new beginning.
My words are everything to me.

If you are offended by reading them
Just imagine how I feel.
If you are encouraged by reading them
Just imagine my healing.

MY CONFESSION LETTER

No one truly knows what happened.
No one truly knows what we did to each other.
No one truly knows how bad things became toward the end.
I am coming out and coming clean.
Here is my confession letter.

I said and did awful things to you.
I attacked you in places that it would hurt the most.
My heart was anxious, fearful, and insecure
So I reacted poorly to everything.
I am coming out and coming clean.
Here is my confession letter.

I hurt you badly.
I was not as innocent as I appeared to be.
I sought terrible council in people who were
Just as broken as I was.
I am coming out and coming clean.
Here is my confession letter.

I made you to be the monster
When it was definitely fifty/fifty.
I am telling everyone what I did
And owning up to my mistakes.
I am coming out and coming clean.
Here is my confession letter.

You tried your best to love me
But I know I am difficult to love.
I made things hard for you
And I will forever carry that burden.
I am coming out and coming clean.
Here is my confession letter.

You are incredible.
You are kind, funny, and generous.
I never deserved someone like you, but you chose me anyway.
I am so sorry that I was awful to you.
I am coming out and coming clean.
Here is my confession letter.

Everyone reading this needs to know
He is an amazing person and was never the bad guy.
I am sorry I led you to believe anything different.
I am coming out and coming clean.
Here is my confession letter.

WHAT I ONCE THOUGHT

What I once thought was a promise from God
Now leaves me more confused and lost.

What I once thought was a promise from God
Now resides as a brutal curse.

What I once thought was a promise from God
Now is just a heavy burden.

What I once thought was a promise from God
Now is a gut-wrenching memory.

What I once thought was a promise from God
Now only feels like a broken one.

MY PAIN: PART 1

I hope one day the pain will pass
From how you moved on so fast.

I guess I am just confused
As to why it was me that feels so hurt and used.

A DAMNED HOLY SAINT

As a Holy Saint
I want to have faith in the promise I think God made me
But it now feels like false hope
That will never happen.

As a Holy Saint
I want to move on, release all unrealistic expectations
And let the anxiety go from the promise I think I got wrong
But it feels like I'm abandoning God.

As a Holy Saint
I simply can't win either way.
I'm damned if I let go and damned if I hold on.
When did being a Christian also mean being a damned Holy Saint?

MY PAIN: PART 2

I can't breathe.
I can't eat.
I can't focus.

My mind is racing.
My heart is beating.
My body is shaking.
My eyes are watering.

I can't breathe.
I can't eat.
I can't focus.

The anxiety is stronger.
The weight is greater.
My body is paralyzed.
I'm being crushed.

I can't breathe.
I can't eat.
I can't focus.

A VOICE THAT HAUNTS

I hear this voice
On repeat in my mind
Saying
"You don't deserve a clean slate."
This haunts me
While chaining me to
Fear
Shame
Guilt and
Worthlessness.

THE SOUNDS OF FEAR

I am scared of
The silence
And I am scared of
The noise.

MAYBE ONE DAY

Maybe one day, I'll write with
Joy in my heart and a
Smile on my face, but
Right now, there is only
Guilt in my soul and
Sadness in my bones.

MY PAIN: PART 3

I wish I could bleed all my emotions out on this page
So my physical pain could mask my emotional pain.

Chapter 2

A Painful death of a once-happy creature

ON THE KITCHEN FLOOR

As I sit on the kitchen floor
My mind racing and my heart pounding
Where are you?

As I sit on the kitchen floor
Crying to the point of no longer breathing
Where are you?

As I sit on the kitchen floor
Holding my knees and shaking uncontrollably
Where are you?

As I sit on the kitchen floor
Losing all sense of hope and reality
Where are you?

As I sit on the kitchen floor
Begging you to show yourself
Where are you?

As I sit on the kitchen floor
Writing this poem
Where are you?

I can tell you where it feels like you're not
And that's on the kitchen floor.

FALLING DOMINOS

The dominos were falling and
We lost control.
Everything we once built
Had come crashing down.
Our destruction hurts, but being
Abandoned to pick up the pieces
Alone hurt the most.

PAINFUL CONSEQUENCES

November fourth meant everything to me.
November fourth nearly destroyed me.

You told me to take a risk and tell my story
But unfortunately, I still only worry.

BROKEN

A broken relationship with
This boy was not my problem
But a broken understanding of
My relationship with the Father.

IS IT WORTH IT?

I'm uncertain.
Everything seems messy
Unstable and
Confusing.
I'm beginning to think
My dreams aren't
Worth all this pain.

UNFORTUNATELY

Self-protection is an attempt to
Avoid pain and hurt
But unfortunately
It mostly causes it.

MY PRISON

The fortress and stronghold
I built to protect myself from fear and hurt
Has now become my prison
Keeping everything out
Including healing from God.

EXPECTING
DISAPPOINTMENT

After being let down so many times
It's hard to expect
Anything other than disappointment.
I'm being hit left and right.
When I stand up, I get knocked right back down.
Dirt is kicked in my face, my eyes are swollen and
My chest is beating.

BATTLE CRY: PART 1

My hands are trembling as I wipe the
Blood, sweat, and tears away.
The world is spinning, and the ground is shifting
Out from under me.
My lungs are giving out, and my sense of reality
Is beginning to fade away.
The ringing in my ears is getting louder
And my throat is aching from screaming.
The smell of smoke and flames fills my body
Staining every bit of me.
I feel smaller and smaller every day, but…

THE MARCH INTO BATTLE

I sense the enemy plotting.
I sense the war coming.
There is something in the air.
My heart is racing.
My stomach is turning
But I look to the sky
Take a breath
And I begin to march.

I hear swords sharpening.
I hear screaming and taunting.
There is something in the air.
My heart is racing.
My stomach is turning
But I quiet my mind
Hum a hymn of praise
And I continue to march.

I feel my body taking a beating.
I feel my soul crying out in agony.
There is something in the air.
My heart is racing.
My stomach is turning
But I stand up straight
Focus my gaze
And I keep on marching.

Chapter 3

A Slight Change in the Wind Brought New Life into Dead Lungs

FLAP OF A
BUTTERFLY'S WING

This morning
I am praying for the winds to change in my life.
I am praying for my circumstances in a different way.
I am praying that my requests would be from a
        place of love and not selfish motives.
I am praying the Lord would check my heart and align it with His.

This morning
The clouds are so low, I could touch them.
They are moving at the speed of light, zipping across the sky.
The weather is changing in one place and
        changed the weather around me.
However, it is more than the weather that was different.

This morning
I see the flap of a butterfly's wing.
One small shift in the wind can cause the whole world to change.
The Lord is working, and the Lord is moving.
Though I cannot see the Spiritual world, I saw a
        glimpse of it in the natural world.

This morning,
The wind is indeed changing in my life, and
        the Lord wants me to know it.

BATTLE CRY: PART 2

I still stand up, strap on my armor
Hold up my shield, raise my sword
And I keep going.
I will fight until I am dead.
I will not be taken captive or made a prisoner.
I will live in freedom or die fighting for it.
And that is all there is to it.

TO BELIEVE OR TO NOT? SO WHY NOT?

Why not believe?
The worst that can happen is that
You are wrong, and your ego is bothered.
What a mere consequence is the
Grand scheme of life.

MY DAUGHTER

My daughter
He may have broken your heart
But let Me be the one to mend it.
Let Me be the one who shows you your true beauty and worth.

THAT'S WHEN GOD

A boy stopped loving me
At my worst
But the funny thing is
That's when God told me
He loved me the most.

I KNOW HE IS THERE

When the world around me
Is spinning out of control
And I cannot seem to get my footing
I know He is there.

When I am drowning
In the sea of pain
And all I feel is anxiety
I know He is there.

When the emotional beatings
Begin to get worse
And I'm covered in bruises and blood
I know He is there.

When players abandon the game
Because a victory seems hopeless
And a loss is all that can be seen
I know He is there.

No matter how uncertain I am
When things get hard
And how defeated I feel
I know He is there.

NOW ON THE
BATTLEFIELD

There is a war being waged on my mind and heart for my soul. I am trying to remain firm in the Father and keep my eyes on Him, but a battlefield can be a brutal place. My thoughts are being bombed with lies, fear, and insecurities. I hear gunshots of future pain, echoing in the distance, quickly getting closer. I hear screaming and yelling as people *attempt* to help me and come to my aid, but they just add to the mayhem. The smell of smoke from everything burning down around me fills my lungs, and I can no longer breathe. My head is ringing, and the whole earth is spinning. I do not know up from down, and everything seems to be uncertain.

With so much chaos and confusion, the reason for the battle is getting lost, but I am gripping it as hard as I can. I am holding tight to the promised victory only found in the Lord, and I'm not letting anyone or anything rip this from my clutch. This war has already been won, but that does not mean I am excused from the fighting. He goes before me, but I am still hanging on His robe, refusing to leave His side. This is where I find safety and comfort.

Right now, I am on the battlefield, sword in hand, ready to swing at the command of the Lord. He has already won it all, but the fight is far from over, but I know who I want and why I want Him. Jesus is my champion and my redeemer. It is Him who I will fight for, it is Him who I will go into war with, and it is Him who I will entrust everything to. He is worth the battle that is being waged on my mind and heart for my soul.

FAITH

Faith is not something that is just handed to you.
Faith is not necessarily a set of beliefs or knowing Truth.
Faith is not something you fully get automatically.

Faith is a conviction you fight for, not something that just happens.
Faith is grown by taking action when you do not want to move.
Faith is cultivated by pausing when you want to run.

Faith is strengthened when the pain never seems to go away.
Faith is living in the reality that God is in
    control, and the war is already won.
Faith is earned with hands open, acknowledging
    they can never do what God can.

Faith is our consistency in a world that is anything but.
Faith is the thing we fall back on when the battle gets hard.
Faith is all we should want because faith is all we need.

TIME

I'm thankful for the past.
I'm content in the present.
I'm hopeful for the future.

GARDENS

If you are doing it right…

Following Jesus is demanding and challenging.
A lot of people think it is like strolling through a flower garden.
And it is
Except it is a garden filled with thorns and thistles
Cutting and slicing as they
Intertwine with the lilies and sunflowers.

Uncertainty and impatience are found in the Garden
But there is also redemption and peace.
Both the good and the bad
Make up the wonderful and magical adventure
Of roaming through the fields
With our kind and loving Father…

If you are doing it right.

CHAPTER 4

A Beautiful Resurrection for a Beautiful Creature

THANK YOU

My sweet Father
Thank You.

Through all the trauma
The pain
And the heartache
You never left my side.

When it felt like
I had lost everything
You remind me
Of how much more I gained.

My sweet Father
Thank You.

BEING REBUILT
FROM THE ASHES

My journey is not about getting over you
Or moving on from what we were
But about discovering myself
And letting the Lord rebuild something beautiful in me
From the wreckage and ashes of what we were.

FREEDOM AT THE ALTAR

I'm finally free.
I gave it up, I gave it all up.
I put everything on the altar and
I'm walking away.

If I was right
Then what a beautiful story of faith that would be.
If I was wrong
Then what a beautiful story of faith that would be.

I'm finally free.
I gave it up, I gave it all up.
I put everything on the altar and
I'm walking away.

AGAIN, I'M IN
THE KITCHEN

Again, I'm in the kitchen
And on my knees
Crying out to the Father
But this time…
This time is different.
My tears are good tears.

I'm no longer sad or angry
But joyful and content.
I'm no longer anxious or fearful
But thankful and forgiven.
I'm no longer broken and shattered
But loved and free.

Again, I'm in the kitchen
And on my knees
Crying out to the Father
But this time…
This time is different.
My tears are good tears.

VOICE OF A FATHER

Oh, how sweet are His words.
It is His voice I listen for every day
For there is no other feeling than hearing
The soft and kind nature of His tone
And the jaw-dropping, earth-shattering power
Of His voice.

HE TELLS ME

He tells me I am more than enough.
He tells me I have a clean slate.
He tells me I am worth the pain of pursuit.
He tells me He will never abandon me.
He tells me these things and promises they will always be true.

A CONFESSIONAL
ACRONYM OF
SYMBOLISM FOR US

Always
Believe
Him
And
Surrender
Everything
Boldly

DANCING

There is something so sweet
So pure about dancing with your
Heavenly Father on the cold, kitchen floor.
Something about it
Is magical and freeing.
Within the twirling and swaying
Nothing is being said, but
Everything is being said.

PROVEN LOVE

When the love of a man
Proved to be conditional
The love of Jesus
Proved to be eternal.

EVERYTHING THAT
WAS EVER LOST

My eyes grew gray and dull
From the pain of betrayal and rejection
But now they are getting their color back
Because the Father heals and restores
Everything that was ever lost.

EPILOGUE

It was a warm day in August. School was about to start, so my best friend and I decided to go hiking in the mountains. We looked up a lot of places to go and decided to try a graveyard hike. It was a bit of a drive to get there, almost two hours, but it was so much fun. We played old music and sang as loud as we could. It was like a dream.

After thoroughly listening to my GPS, we arrived at our destination, except there was nothing there. We drove around for half an hour, looking for anything and finding nothing. We gave up and decided to just drive around the area and see what there was to do. Then, we found a river where all kinds of sketchy people were fishing and swimming. There was a trail, or at least we thought it was a trail, and decided to explore.

The entire time, we are laughing, making jokes, and having the time of our lives. He was my best friend. We did everything together. During our very first shift at work, we hit it off fast. Everyone associated us together. It got to the point he would make jokes like, "I will never date anyone so I can be your best friend forever." That was us, best friends for life.

While exploring, we found a clearing in the woods. It was probably one of the most creepy and eerie places I have ever been to. Covering the area were millions of dead butterflies. Some looked like they had taken a beating from animals and the weather. Some looked as if their last breath was just a second ago. You couldn't even see the ground because of all the dead butterflies. After being there for two minutes, we dipped out. It was gross and unsettling.

After we left, he drove my car to this lookout point. This was a long and rocky road that took us well over an hour to drive. He almost bottomed out my car several times and came close to blowing a tire. On the way up, we kept asking each other questions. It was one of the most personal and intimate conversations we had ever had. While listening to Jack and Diane, The Joker, and all the Temptations and Elton John songs, we got to know each other. We asked questions for hours.

The top of the mountain was beautiful, I closed my eyes, and I still saw the breathtaking view. We set up our Enos and sat for hours. We kept asking about each other's lives—the deep and personal stuff. We connected that day, and our friendship was never the same.

All the way home, we continued to laugh. Oh, my goodness, we laughed so hard. He drove my car back to his house, which kind of bummed us both out because we didn't want the day to end. But he had dinner at his grandmother's house, so he was pretty hype about that. He loves his family so much. It's admirable.

Now I know what you're thinking, where does this go bad? Fast forward a few months and we're dating. I swore I was going to marry him. Being with him felt right, but no matter how much two people love and care for each other, the pain and baggage from the past will always catch up if they're never dealt with. That's our story. We were two broken humans who fell in love, ripped apart by the pain we inflicted on each other.

I think about the Butterfly Graveyard every day. What used to be a memory that filled me with joy and peace now brings regret and pain because he and I are no longer together. We're no longer friends. We no longer talk. Our current relationship is so bad that it physically causes me pain. More than anything, I miss my best friend. I miss him so much. But there is so much trauma between us. I fear we will never be okay. The memory of the Butterfly Graveyard haunted me with anxiety and failure.

I didn't write this to glamorize what happened. I wrote this to heal and share my story. I brought into the relationship wounds that I didn't know I had until we started to date. These wounds only got bigger and deeper as they were exposed. We dated through the Spring that COVID-19 hit. It was during that time I lost a safe home, and I lost my mental and physical health, which were factors in losing him.

After the breakup, I lost my job and most of my friends. All of this contributed to my internal death. I physically was alive, but I was completely dead on the inside. I lost myself. Instead of attempting to heal these wounds, I let them fester and worsen until there was nothing left of me. I didn't know any better. I was dumb and naive, but now I understand. I'm beginning to see outside myself now.

This is my story of God's redemption and healing through poetry. And this is not just healing from a broken relationship but years of trauma, heartache, abuse, and self-sabotage. I was knocked down, but I kept getting back up, and now I'm a different person because of it. This is my resurrection from broken and shriveled up to strong and whole. This is my story of how I wrestled with God about the purpose of suffering. This is the resurrection of my Butterfly Graveyard.

Less than two years later, after the Butterfly Graveyard adventure, the sun was setting, and it began to rain. My mom and I sat on the front porch, just talking about life after a relaxing Mother's Day spent together. We talked about this book, specifically the "Epilogue." At the time, I had no idea where I was going with this. I felt frustrated and hopeless. I was also angry and spiteful. In all honesty, I could not think of anything happy to write or celebrate. I believed that the anger in my heart protected me from future pain and harm. I hated the fact that I still love him, but I believed that there were too many wounds inflicted for me and my best friend to be restored.

I believed God took everything from me because I let Him down. I believed, much like the original Israelites in the wilderness, I lost the promise from God, and that was it. Then my mom told me I was living by the law and not by grace. She said, "You wouldn't believe this for anyone else, but you're keeping yourself captive to a lie." An amazing thing about Jesus is that He sets prisoners free. He gives second chances. He restores and redeems everything that is lost and broken. *Resurrecting the Butterfly Graveyard* is my story, wrestling with the Lord to learn His voice, my worth, and what true authentic healing looks like. It's about learning to sit with God during suffering and pain.

There are forty poems in this book. The number forty represents trials, tribulation, or a period of testing. So there are forty poems to represent my wandering, waiting, and testing. These forty poems are about learning to truly live in freedom and wrestling with God and myself to get there.

I want to leave you with the idea of internal healing versus external healing. My mom suggested I write about a cocoon and the beautiful process of metamorphosis. Though I loved this idea, I wanted my story to go a little deeper. A caterpillar turning into a butterfly is an external process, but a dead butterfly resurrecting is an internal change because new breath fills its lungs. Butterflies transition all the time, but resurrections are special miracles from God.

The rest of my journey, not written in this book, is the discipline of learning to die to my disappointment and bitterness and let the Lord resurrect my heart in faith and love. I'm learning to let go of all the hate and walk in forgiveness and hope. It's a daily decision, and some days I know I won't pick this, but I'm choosing to believe that making this a habit will eventually become my lifestyle.

My dream is that the Lord redeems and heals me and my best friend. My dream is for the Lord to mend what was broken in us. My dream is that the Lord restores my identity and my shattered heart. And also, my dream is to be joyful with God even if I can't have what I want. Though this book has come to an end, this journey has not. Life is not easy, and God never claimed it would be. However, He did say that He loves unconditionally and will never ever leave our side.

Sitting on the cool, rainy porch, I thought that this truth wasn't enough. My mom reminded me it's more than enough and, in fact, way more than we deserve. God is still resurrecting but won't do anything without my best attempt at being faithful. The Butterfly Graveyard no longer has a bitter place in my heart. I use it as a litmus test to see how much the Lord has done in my heart and how much more He wants to do. In fact, I wear a butterfly pendant around my neck to remind me that He's still resurrecting the metaphorical dead butterflies in the graveyard of my heart.

AN EXCERPT FROM "MY ONE-YEAR STORY"

Anxiety, pain, and fear consumed every thought. I remember telling my counselor, Morgan (who is also a dear friend), that I was spiraling and could not make a good decision to save my life. I allowed the enemy to speak lies over me. He told me that I was not worth a clean slate, that I was too much and too selfish, and that I believed every word. I allowed the poor advice of friends to dictate my life, instead of relying on the truth-saturated words of the Father. It was so bad. Having a quiet time or watching church would cause a panic attack because I was reminded of the person that I hurt so deeply.

Between 2019 and 2021, the Lord took me on an incredible journey. I went from being the most unstable I have ever been to a much healthier, happier, and hope-filled person. Despite who I used to be, the Lord never saw me as being expendable but, instead, as someone who is worthy, someone who deserves a clean slate. He had to take everything away from me, everything that I held on tightly to for identity. The Father took my identity in serving and ministry. He took my identity in my job. He took my identity in school. He took my identity as being independent. He also took my identity as being codependent. He unraveled the yarn of lies, sewing me into something brand new.

Because the Lord has been creating something beautiful from my ashes, He created a sense of "full circle" in my life. He took my prideful nature of serving and turned it into a humble calling in writing. He took my arrogant nature of succeeding in school and has given me eyes to see it's not about me. He took my old job that I was good at, compromised it, and now has given me a new one with the most loving and kind people. He took my old apartment and self-given independence and taught me to be dependent on Him. Funny thing is, I am living in my old apartment complex, with my new bedroom looking down at my old one. Symbolically, the Lord used this to show how much I have grown and that I am not where I used to be but have gone higher with Him.

God is giving everything I lost back to me but even more beautiful. My battle with anxiety has never been this good, my health has never been better (both mental and physical), and I have never been happier and more hopeful for the future. I'm learning who I am and who God created me to be. In this season of getting to know the Lord in an intimate and vulnerable way, He now speaks to me in ways that He has never spoken to me before. I hear His voice. I know His voice. I feel His presence. I feel the company of the angelic army. I am not just following Jesus now, but I am relationally doing life with Him. I no longer have panic attacks in the presence of God, but I jump out of bed excited to spend time with Him. Now every car ride is a worship and prayer session. Jesus is no longer a part of my life but is my whole life.

The idea of faith is what changed everything for me. Hebrews 11:1 (NIV) says, "Now faith is the assurance of things hoped for, the conviction of things not seen." Because of everything this past year, I now understand what faith is. It is believing in something that cannot be seen in the natural world but only in your heart. Despite how bad everything was, I would not change a thing because I now have a deep and genuine faith that God is who He says He is. I will forever put my faith in God and God alone. I know that He has promised good things to me. He has promised a life of redemption, restoration, and healing. Who I used to be does not define me, but it serves as a launchpad to the person the Lord is calling me to be. I love who I am and who He is making me to be. I know I am loved. I am forgiven. I am redeemed. I am restored. I am healed. No one will ever be able to tell me any different ever again.

Behind me are piles of ashes from burned bridges and torched relationships, but the Lord can breathe life into anything and grow the most beautiful gardens. My story is not pretty. My story is not ideal. My story is not how I wanted it to look, but my story is not over. I have a lifetime of growth with the Lord, learning how to be loved, learning to love like Him, and being reminded daily to place everything on the altar and walk away. Faith is not easy, but faith is all I have now. I am choosing to believe that something better than I could ever imagine is coming.

ABOUT THE AUTHOR

Sarah Elizabeth Beach was born in the low country of South Carolina but grew up in the upstate. She has a certificate of completion from NewSpring Leadership College in student ministry and her bachelor's degree in Christian ministry and apologetics from Anderson University. She has two wonderful parents and an amazing little sister. Her debut book is *Resurrecting the Butterfly Graveyard* though she was published in A Celebration of Poets when in high school.

She has been writing since elementary school, specifically telling stories. She loves using poetry to create a work of art within the mind. Like a painting can stir emotions in the viewer, Sarah Elizabeth wants to use her words to do the same. Her poetry shares stories that connect hearts and create a mental image of feeling emotions with God.

Her writing is real, vulnerable, and authentic. Sarah Elizabeth's dream is to help people become closer to God by tapping into their emotions and processing them with the Holy Spirit. All of her writing points back to the Lord and walking an incredible journey with Him.

9 798886 166071